Railways & Recollections 1975

Contents

Series Introduction

Railway publishing has been around almost as long as the railways themselves and there have been countless books with a historical theme, telling the story of a particular line, say, and occasionally linking the subject to its social context, but never before has there been, in such an accessible way, a juxtapositioning of photographic illustration of a railway subject with the events, happenings and highlights of a wider sphere and calendar. This series will, initially, take a particular year and place the views displayed alongside a carefully selected pot-pourri of what happened in that twelve-month period. The vast majority of the images in the first few books are from the Ray Ruffell collection, held by the publisher, but material from other sources will be interspersed where felt necessary to maintain appropriate variety. Ray was a railwayman and photographer of equal merit and the main criterion for inclusion in these books is for the images to be both interesting and aesthetically pleasing within a chosen theme.

The books are aimed at a more general market than mere railway aficionados or enthusiasts and the authors hope and trust that they will be sure in their aim and that you, the reader, will find much to enjoy, appreciate, enthuse about and even smile about! And it is hoped that some of your own memories are stirred along the way and that you may wish to share these with friends!

© Peter Townsend and John Stretton 2008
Photos: © The NOSTALGIA Collection archive unless otherwise credited.

First published in 2008
ISBN 978 1 85794 294 1
Silver Link Publishing Ltd
The Trundle
Ringstead Road
Great Addington
Kettering
Northants NN14 4BW

Tel/Fax: 01536 330588
email: sales@nostalgiacollection.com
Website: www.nostalgiacollection.com
British Library Cataloguing in Publication Data
A catalogue record for this book is available from the British Library.
Printed and bound in Great Britain

Frontispiece: **READING:** On a day of fluctuating weather conditions, the sun has appeared to attractively highlight 'Class 47' No 47245 as it heads the distinctly mixed 8E40 freight from the north towards the station complex. New in December 1966 as D1922 to Cardiff (Canton) shed it became 47245 in October 1973 and subsequently bore the names *Linnet* (unofficially) and *The Institute of Export.* At the time of writing it was still on the stocks under the control of Riviera Trains.

Opposite background **CROWTHORNE:** The last week of March in our year saw significant snowfall in the Southern half of the country. On Thursday 27 March, the photographer's young daughter endures the bitter cold conditions to witness an unidentified inter regional parcels working behind 'Class 33' No 33045.

Introduction

Undoubtedly, the key event of 1975 in World terms was the ending of the Vietnam War with the evacuation of the very last American troops from Saigon on 30 April. The war had 'initially ended' with the signing of a peace treaty in Paris on 27 January 1973 but violations continued throughout 1974. Not until Premier Nguyen Van Thieu of South Vietnam resigned and the South Vietnamese Government surrendered to the North Vietnamese did the war finally draw to a close. Other events involving the US included two assassination attempts on President Ford and the 'Watergate Cover Up' trial, resulting in guilty verdicts for defendants John N. Mitchell, H. R. Haldeman & John D. Ehrlichman. On a more positive note the US *Apollo* and Russian *Soyuz 19* space crafts linked-up in space.

Nearer home 1975 was the year in which Margaret Thatcher defeated Edward Heath to become leader of the Conservative Party and the Country voted to stay in the European Community in a referendum. The Channel Tunnel was again in the news as work was abandoned on the latest attempt to span the channel divide. Harold Wilson, the British PM, called a halt as an economy measure.

On the rails in 1975 there were many highs and lows. British Rail's Advanced Passenger Train achieved a speed of over 150mph on the Western Region main line between Goring and Uffington and the new National Railway Museum was officially opened by Prince Phillip, Duke of Edinburgh on 27 September. It was the first full year of TOPS, with most locomotives judged to have a long enough life being renumbered; but it was the last year for Beyer Peacock Type 3 'Hymeks', with just six from the original class of 101 making it into this year. The last examples were dispensed with in March.

Two major accidents occurred; the first, on 28 February at Moorgate tube station on the London Underground, resulted in over 40 fatalities as the train ran into the buffers at this terminus station. The second involved the 23.30 London Euston to Glasgow sleeper which was delayed by engine failure, resulting in it running an hour behind schedule. On approaching Nuneaton a vital advance notice speed restriction sign was not illuminated and on reaching the second sign the train was travelling at a speed from which, in spite of emergency brakes being applied, it could not slow sufficiently to avoid being derailed at the track remodelling taking place just short of Nuneaton station. The ensuing carnage resulted in the death of two staff and four passengers with over thirty others being injured. In the US, three restored steam locomotives hauled the second *Freedom Train*, the first having run in 1947-1949. The train carried around 500 items of treasured Americana ranging from George Washington's copy of the Constitution to Joe Fraziers's boxing trunks! The train set off from Wilmington, Delaware on 1 April and ran through 48 States, attracting over seven million visitors before ending its long haul in Miami, Florida on 31 December 1976.

In the world of film *Jaws* was scaring audiences to the extent that it was the highest grossing film of the year. The major awards, however, went to the thought provoking *One Flew Over The Cuckoo's Nest* starring *Jack Nicholson*. Not since 1934 (*It Happened One Night*) had a film won all five major Academy Awards.

1975 was an interesting year musically with Led Zeppelin selling out three concerts at Madison Square Garden in a record 4 hours after tickets went on sale. (Interestingly, an estimated 20 million people tried to secure a ticket for the group's one-off reunion concert at London's O2 venue on 26 November 2007!!!). The Who's now famous musical *Tommy* premiered in London and Queen's *Bohemian Rhapsody* climbed to number 1 in the US charts and stayed there for nine weeks.
Once again, your two authors have derived enormous pleasure in compiling the enclosed selection of images and we trust you will share that enjoyment in this latest volume in the series...

Peter Townsend
Northamptonshire
February 2008

John Stretton
Gloucestershire

SALISBURY On 29 May 'Class 52' No D1068 *Western Reliance* departs with the 1A83 stone train to Botley. This is one of the Crewe built 'Westerns', having been outshopped in July 1963: she was withdrawn in October of 1976.

Inset: **READING** Brass rubbing is by no means confined to ecclesiastical subjects! A group of enthusiasts set to work, quickly(!) on 'Class 52' No 1069 *Western Vanguard* as she pauses at Reading with a London bound service.

Opposite: **READING** With the appalling weather echoing the sombre occasion, Laira based 'Class 52' D1054 *Western Governor* awaits departure from Reading with a London bound train as fellow Diesel Hydraulic, 'Class 35' Hymek No D7017, one of only four still in service, runs though light engine. This shot was taken on 18 March and by the end of the month all the Hymeks were withdrawn. D7017 was to be one of four lucky ones being saved from the cutter's torch - she was, at the time of writing, undergoing a major repair at The West Somerset Railway.

Western Twilight

Left: **READING** On the left, on 28 August, in Platform 4B, the 12.32 departure for London Waterloo is in the hands of Set 7422. Meanwhile set 1201 waits in Platform 4A, rostered as the 12.26 to Tonbridge and 'Class 52' D1026 *Western Centurion* is in charge of the 1V28 fast train to Paddington over in Platform 5.

Below: **READING** Moments later Set 1201 is still awaiting the off as 'Class 52' D1026 *Western Centurion* limps into the station with the 1V28 train, her twin Maybach engines' exhaust plume being reminiscent of the steam age railway!

READING Despite being the subject of at least two cameras, on 28 August, D1055 *Western Advocate* looks to be in serious need of tender loving care (TLC) as she awaits departure for London Paddington with the 1V28 service, having taken over from the ailing D1026. Sadly TLC was in short supply and she had but a short time to live, being withdrawn in January 1976 and scrapped at Swindon shortly after. Nearest the camera is set 1201 still awaiting departure with the 12.26 to Tonbridge.

1975
Sporting Highlights

Wimbledon
The singles winners were:
Men's Singles Final: Arthur Ashe beats
Jimmy Connors to win
6-1, 6-1, 5-7, 6-4 after 125 minutes in an all
USA final

Mrs L. W. King (USA) beats Miss R. A.
Cawley (AUS) to win Women's Singles
Final:
6-0, 6-1 in just 38 Minutes!

Motor Racing
Niki Lauda wins the F1 Championship with
Ferrari

Golf
Jack Nicklaus wins his fifth Masters and
fourth PGA Championship

The FA Cup 1975
West Ham United win 2 - 0 against
Fulham at Wembley

The League Cup 1975 (over two legs)
Aston Villa beat Norwich 1 - 0

The Football League Champions
Derby County

Above: **READING** 'Class 47' No 47378 a Cardiff based loco at this time (18 March) passes through with a long rake of cement wagons. DANGER DON'T TOUCH THE CONDUCTOR RAILS reads the notice - very sensible advice! The Southern Railway had its own terminus at Reading for its third rail electric trains but following closure on 6 September 1965, Southern region trains were diverted to platform 4A, initially, of the Great Western station. The conductor rails being limited to that platform road.

Opposite left: **READING** The driver of Old Oak Common based 'Class 50' No 50001 passes the time of day with Joan Ruffell as he awaits departure from Reading on 18 March with a Bristol bound express. Originally numbered D401 this locomotive, built at Vulcan Foundry, entered service on the West Coast Main Line in December 1967 and in later years carried the name *Dreadnought,* applied at Laira Depot in April 1978.

Right: **READING** 'Class 47' No 47081 *Odin* draws into Reading with an up express on 18 March. Built at Crewe and released to traffic in March 1965 this loco carried the original number D1666 and was sent new to Swansea's Landore shed. When this view was taken she was based at Old Oak Common. She subsequently carried the numbers 47606 (twice!) 47842 and finally 47778. She was named *Odin* for most of her 41 year life but also carried *Irresistible* and *Duke of Edinburgh's Award* when numbered 47778. Her end came in March 2006 at EMR Kingsbury.

READING On April Fools Day 'Class 47' No 47138 a Bristol Bath Road based loco takes centre stage having just arrived with the 16.25 service from Oxford. At the opposite platform stands SR set 7386 forming the 17.00 departure for London Waterloo and in the bay to the right 'Class 33' No 33029 is in charge of the 17.07 service to Redhill. Plans were announced during 2007 for the dramatic remodelling of Reading station, to enhance and ease traffic flows between the cross country route and the West of England main line.

READING On 19 November this service from Birmingham going forward to London Paddington should have been hauled by a 'Class 52' Western. The reason for the non appearance was not known but the sight of a double header was always a bonus and on this occasion it is hauled by two 'Class 31's in the form of Nos 31265 and 31260. At the head of the train, 31265 later, after withdrawal, became something of a celebrity. Having been renumbered 31430, on conversion to a 31/4

when ETH equipment was fitted and it was moved to Bescot TMD, a subsequent transfer to infrastructure duties as 31530 saw it painted in 'Dutch' livery before withdrawal in January 1999. Preservation then beckoned with it arriving at Dereham, on The Mid Norfolk Railway, on Monday 9 December 2002. While at Bescot it was named '*Sister Dora*' after the

famous Walsall Nursing Sister. (Readers may like to know that Sister Dora features in *Hidden Gems of the Black Country* published by Silver Link, from which the illustration of the plaque *below* is taken).

READING On 15 October this view of Reading station taken from the London end shows to good effect the extensive layout at this busy station on the Great Western Main Line. However the original Great Western station is now also home to the old Southern Railway services on the Reading to Waterloo and/or Redhill and Brighton line, from this side of the station. Meanwhile at the 'Bristol' end services depart to Basingstoke, Salisbury and Portsmouth, which became part of British Railways Southern Region, following Nationalisation of the railways in 1948.

Above: **READING** On 11 August 1975 a glimpse of the future passes through Reading! This is prototype HST set No 252 001 built during 1972 and delivered in August of that year. The complete set consisted of seven coaches and two power cars, variations in formation running extensive trials on the Western Region until 1976. These shots of a formation with just 3 carriages and 2 power cars are, therefore, relatively late in the trial period. Indeed the first production power car was delivered in late 1975 and the first public services commenced in October 1976 between Paddington and Bristol/South Wales. By May of 1977 the HST had replaced all loco hauled expresses on the Paddington to South Wales route.

Above: **READING** The railway system is not occupied solely by regulation passenger or freight vehicles. Over the years there has been all manor of stock improving, regulating and or inspecting the infrastructure. On 16 October, a Speno International rail grinding train visiting from Switzerland stands in the yard of Reading Diesel Depot.

Left: **READING** We have already referred to the closure of Reading South station 10 years earlier and transfer of traffic to platforms 4A and 4B at Reading General. The construction of this latter platform is seen on 12 February. Most enthusiasts would not have taken this shot and this is again credit to Ray Ruffel's foresight and wide interest.

DIDCOT On 30 March the Great Western Railway Centre at Didcot were holding an Open Day and for the Ruffells it was a family day out. Mother and daughter watch from the main line station as visitors make their way to the entrance to the steam centre. '7800' Class 4-6-0 No 7808 *Cookham Manor* is seen in the distance hauling two auto-coaches. This loco was built at Swindon in 1938 and became part of The Great Western Society's fleet as early as 1966. Like a number of its stable mates the 'Manor' has been in preservation longer than it was in service on GWR/BR metals.

DIDCOT Developed as a junction between the Great Western main line and the route striking north through Oxford and Banbury to Birmingham, Wolverhampton and, ultimately, Chester, Didcot rapidly became an important and bustling centre for marshalling freight trains. On 30 March, on the left of the picture a 350HP BR 'Class 08' shunter awaits its next turn of duty, whilst to its right, locomotives from 'Classes 47 and 31' stand in line. 6Z96 rests with a loaded 'merry-go-round' coal train destined for the infamous Power Station seen in the background.

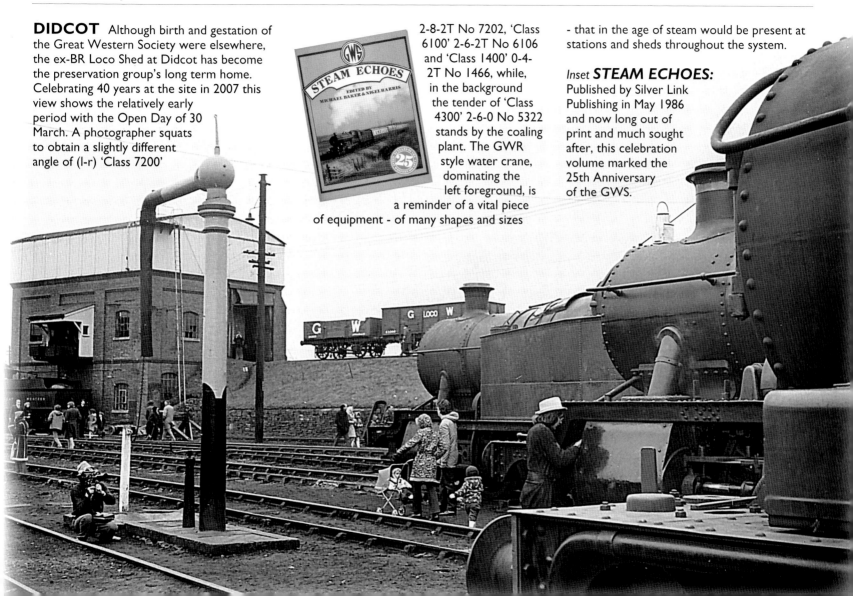

DIDCOT Although birth and gestation of the Great Western Society were elsewhere, the ex-BR Loco Shed at Didcot has become the preservation group's long term home. Celebrating 40 years at the site in 2007 this view shows the relatively early period with the Open Day of 30 March. A photographer squats to obtain a slightly different angle of (l-r) 'Class 7200'

2-8-2T No 7202, 'Class 6100' 2-6-2T No 6106 and 'Class 1400' 0-4-2T No 1466, while, in the background the tender of 'Class 4300' 2-6-0 No 5322 stands by the coaling plant. The GWR style water crane, dominating the left foreground, is a reminder of a vital piece of equipment - of many shapes and sizes - that in the age of steam would be present at stations and sheds throughout the system.

Inset **STEAM ECHOES:** Published by Silver Link Publishing in May 1986 and now long out of print and much sought after, this celebration volume marked the 25th Anniversary of the GWS.

1975 Arrivals & Departures

Births

Edith Bowman	*disc jockey*		15 January
Keith Gillespie	*footballer*		18 February
Gary Neville	*footballer*		18 February
Drew Barrymore	*actress*		22 February
Robbie Fowler	*footballer*		9 April
David Beckham	*footballer*		2 May
Enrique Inglesias	*singer*		8 May
Jonah Lomu	*rugby player*		12 May
John Higgins	*snooker player*		18 May
Jamie Oliver	*chef*		27 May
Angelina Jolie	*actress*		4 June
Jill Halfpenny	*actress*		15 July
Kate Winslet	*actress*		5 October
Ronnie O'Sullivan	*snooker player*		5 December
Tiger Woods	*golfer*		30 December

Deaths

P.G. Wodehouse	*English writer*	(b. 1881)	14 February
Susan Hayward	*actress*	(b. 1917)	14 March
Aristotle Onassis	*shipping magnate*	(b. 1906)	15 March
King Faisal of Saudi Arabia	*actor*	(b. 1906)	25 March
William Hartnell	*actor*	(b. 1908)	23 April
Eamon de Valera	*3rd Irish President*	(b. 1882)	29 August
Haile Selassie I	*Ethiopian Emperor*	(b. 1892)	27 September
Graham Hill	*racing driver*	(b. 1929)	29 November

DIDCOT: Walking round and or just standing watching at a large site like that of the GWS at Didcot can be tiring, not least for an 'enthusiast's nearest and dearest'. Here the photographer's wife and daughter take refuge on a bench seat, along with other visitors, to watch ex-GWR 2-6-2T No 6106 pass on its auto-coach shuttle.

There is a wide range of age groups in evidence here and of course, this is encouraging, as the future of preservation will ultimately lie in the hands of upcoming generations who will not recall the days when steam ruled the rails. Who knows, many of the youngsters illustrated in these pages could well now be taking their own children to Didcot!

DIDCOT Still during the Open Day of 30 March, two of the three locomotives seen 'from behind' on page 17 are again in view here, this time from a more standard vantage point. In the centre 'Manor Class' 4-6-0 No 7808 *Cookham Manor* has replaced 6106 from the view seen earlier, and is now resting after duties on the shuttle line. One of the major attractions of the site is evidenced by this picture, being the facility of 'getting up close and personal' to the resident locomotives. In the background - coded 81E in BR days - the old steam shed, with ancient fan light ventilators, still serves its former purpose but now for locomotives in receipt of much greater TLC. Were you there? What happened to the fashion for platform soled shoes (appropriate attire for a railway location?)

1975 TV Favourites a selection

Celebrity Squares (ATV/ITV)
Bob Monkhouse hosted game show first of initial run of 138 episodes broadcast in July

Dad's Army (BBC)
The eighth series of 6 episodes plus a Christmas special of the popular look at life in The Home Guard

Doctor Who (BBC)
Tom Baker, the fourth Doctor, encounters the birth of the Daleks amongst the year's adventures.

Fawlty Towers (BBC)
The start of the legendary shows starring John Cleese, Prunella Scales, Andrew Sachs and Connie Booth.

Jim'll Fix It (BBC)
First transmitted on 31 May 1975, (Sir) Jimmy Saville fixed it for lucky people selected from the huge numbers of letters received.

The Sweeney (ABC)
The first episode *Ringer* transmits on 2 January

The Naked Civil Servant (ITV)
Screened on 17 December, this 85 minute film of the life of Quentin Crisp, played by John Hurt, took the nation by storm winning a Best Actor BAFTA for John Hurt.

DIDCOT Another view of the GWS site and its enthusiastic and excited visitors to the 30 March Open Day shows some extent of the shed yard. In the left foreground 'Class 4300' 4MT 2-6-0 No 5322 is positioned by the coaling tower, with one of the small loading tugs poised ready to deposit its load of, one would hope, finest quality South Wales coal, much favoured by the GWR, into the tender. The Churchward designed freight type was originally introduced in 1911 and gave around half a century of valuable service to the railway.

DIDCOT Locomotives Nos 5322 *(foreground)* and 6106 *(in the distance giving rides on the shuttle line)* have already been seen. Another exhibit for this Open Day on 30 March, taking centre stage, but not in steam, is 'Class 5600' 0-6-2T No 6697. Originally introduced in 1924 - and designated 5MT by virtue of its power - this Collett type was designed for service in the Welsh Valleys. No doubt hauling that prized Welsh coal round the many tight curves in the area for which this loco type was particularly well suited. 6697 was one of the slightly later type, with detail alterations and being slightly heavier, introduced in 1927.

DIDCOT Our final view of the Open Day of 30 March gives us a much wider panorama of the GWS' shed yard. The locomotives standing outside the shed building have been seen already, whilst, to the left, we have an addition to the day's selection. 'Hall Class' 4-6-0 No. 6998 *'Burton Agnes Hall'* heads a rake of the Society's coaching stock, simulating the arrival of a visiting train. Over the years, the extreme left of this view has changed dramatically, with 'hard standing' installed to the left of the rails and both cafe and museum buildings erected for the pleasure and satisfaction of visitors.

CHESTER One often high profile feature
of our erstwhile railway system that has been
eliminated from much of the current system
is the signalbox. Swept away by the advent
of modern technology and the introduction
of colour lights to replace the 'old fashioned'
semaphore arms, many of the installations
were both aesthetically attractive and gems of
railway architectural engineering. One such
was the No. 6 Box at Chester, seen from the
10.00 Euston-Bangor express of 12 April. Old
style lighting, semaphore signal and terraced
housing all complete the picture. 'Class 47' No
47474, at the head of the train, was built at
Crewe and was new from July 1964 as D1602.
Renumbered in February 1974, under BR's
TOPS system, it acquired the name *Sir Rowland
Hill* in 1990, before being withdrawn in late
2005 and scrapped at T J Thomson , Stockton
on Tees on 2 November of that year.

LOCATION MAP

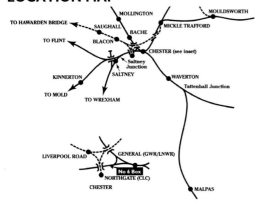

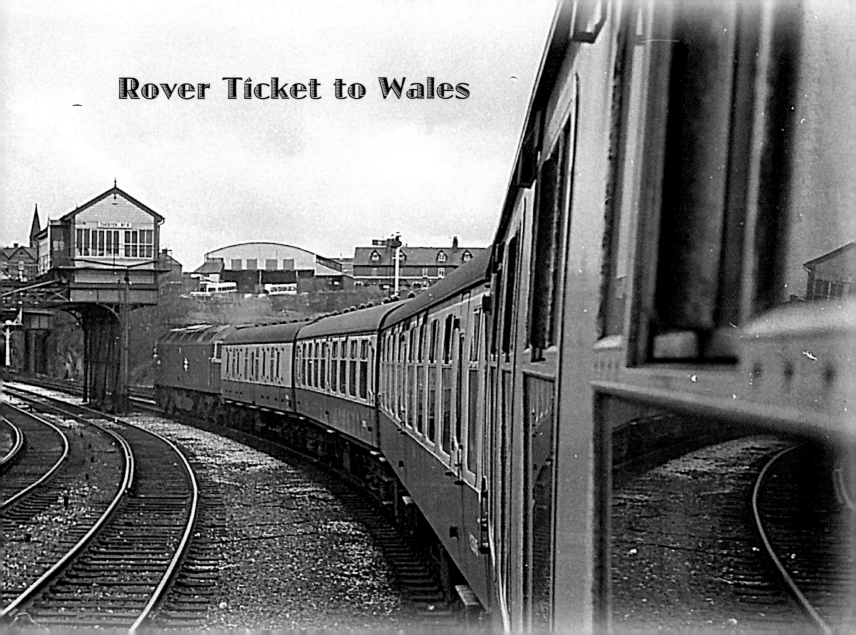

Rover Ticket to Wales

CONWAY On 12 April, 'Class 47' No 47474 heads into the 'tunnel' of the Conway Tubular Bridge, about to pass Conwy Castle, at the head of the already seen 10.00 Euston-Bangor express. Seen from the fourth coach of the train, evidence of years of smoke from steam engines entering the bridge can be seen on the castellated walls, with the castle battlements to the right and, right foreground, piles of recently uprooted and neatly stacked specially designed track fixings taken from the bridge. Note the more modern, utilitarian railway office building by the trackside.

CHESTER: Going back to Chester we now have another view from the 10.00 Euston-Bangor express, this time showing the diesel depot as the train left the station earlier in the day. The units from left to right are: Gloucester RC&W 1960-built 'Class 128' Parcels Car, Gloucester RC&W 1957-built 'Class 100' two-car unit and two Metro-Cammell 'Class 101s' on the right.

1975
Happenings (1)

January
- Watergate verdict finds defendents John Ehrlichman, John Mitchell and Harry Haldeman guilty of cover up.
- Work abandoned by Britain on the latest Channel Tunnel on financial grounds.
- Dr Donald Coggan becomes 101st Archbishop of Canterbury.
- Donald Nielsen abducts Leslie Whittle from Shropshire home.

February
- Margaret Thatcher succeeds Edward Heath as Conservative Party leader
- Moorgate Tube crash kills 41 people
- New £10 note issued by the Royal Mint featuring the H M The Queen on the front and Florence Knightingale on the reverse.
- P.G.Wodehouse dies at the age of 93 in Remsenburg, USA.

March
- Charlie Chaplin knighted by the H M The Queen at Buckingham Palace on a rare visit to the UK.
- The USSR and the USA carry out underground nuclear tests.
- Leslie Whittle found dead at the bottom of a drain shaft.
- Colour TV broadcasts begin in Australia.

Background **THE MOON:** NO NOT REALLY! We are on the way up to the summit of Snowdon aboard The Snowdon Mountain Railway on 15 April with a view from Clogwyn looking down to LLyn Du'r Arddu.

Inset below **AFON HWCH VIADUCT:** Many of the thousands of visitors to The Snowdon Mountain Railway each year are either unaware that the locomotive is pushing their train up the hill or have not given consideration as to why this should be. Following the one accident in the railways history shortly after opening, this mode of operation was adopted to prevent any possibility of a run away train. On 15 April No 4 *Snowdon* pushes its train on the approach to the viaduct in bright spring sunshine.

Inset above **PENLLYN:** Once the preserve of local quarrying, the Llanberis Lake Railway now occupies the lakeside trackbed. On 16 April, *Elidir* stands at the Penllyn terminus, shortly before running round its train for the return trip to Gilfach Ddu.

1975
Happenings (2)

April
- Vietnam War ends as the Capital - Saigon falls to North Vietnamese troops.

May
- England beat Scotland 5-1 at Wembley in the home internationals
- Flixborough Inquiry published. Finds bypass pipe failed due to unforeseen lateral stresses.

June
- The Suez Canal is re-opened by Egypt's President Sadat
- British people vote in first ever referendum and decide (67.2% in favour) to stay in the EEC
- Inquest finds, in his absence, Lord Lucan guilty of murdering nanny Sandra Rivett.
- First North Sea oil from the British sector comes ashore at BP's Refinery on the Isle of Grain
- First live radio broadcast from House of Commons

July
- American *Apollo* and Russian *Soyuz* space craft dock in space - astronauts shake hands!
- American president Gerald Ford visits the Nazi Concentration Camp at Auschwitz.

August
- The *Birmingham Six* are wrongfully sentenced to Life Imprisonment.
- The ailing British Leyland is nationalised.

Above: **NEW ROMNEY** Power in miniature outside New Romney shed. On the left is 4-6-2 *Hurricane* built in 1927 by Davey Paxman & Co. This was, reportedly, for many years Captain Howey, the RHDR founder's favourite locomotive. On the right sister locomotive also built by Davey Paxman & Co in 1927, but with an additional set of driving wheels, 4-8-2 *Sampson.* stands ready to go off shed for her next turn of duty.

Opposite lower: **NEW ROMNEY** Moving the camera to the right reveals 4-6-2 *Typhoon* built in 1927 and delivered to the RHDR in May of that year. She was built, like *Hurricane*, with three cylinders in an effort to increase the power and speed over the previously delivered 'Pacifics' *Green Goddess, Northern Chief* and *Southern Maid.* The experiment was however troublesome and the benefits were outweighed by the increased running costs and in 1935-6 she was converted to the proven two cylinder arrangement.

Below: **NEW ROMNEY** The driver's eye view aboard 4-6-2 *Green Goddess,* approaching New Romney with the 15.20 departure from Hythe on 25 June. This was one of two locomotives ordered by Count Louis Zborowski, Captain Howey's original partner in the plan for an express narrow gauge railway that was eventually to come to fruition as the RHDR. Sadly Count Louis Zborowski did not live to see the finished dream. A well known racing driver of his time, and an early investor in the Aston Martin car company he was killed at Monza while taking part in the Italian Grand Prix on 19 October 1924. *Green Goddess* was delivered in 1925 and as the RHDR was not yet open Captain Howey arranged for the locomotive to visit The Ravenglass & Eskdale

The Romney, Hythe & Dymchurch Railway

Railway for running in and testing. The two railways have co-operated with each other ever since with many locomotives travelling in both directions for special events, galas and celebrations. *Green Goddess* is at the time of writing out of service undergoing a major overhaul; the old lady is now over 80 years old so she deserves a well earned break and TLC!

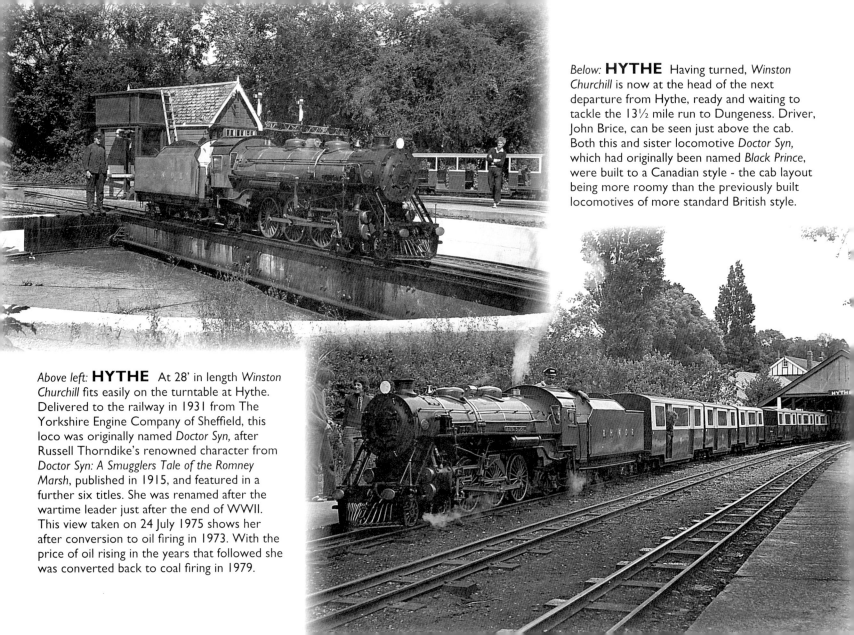

Below: **HYTHE** Having turned, *Winston Churchill* is now at the head of the next departure from Hythe, ready and waiting to tackle the 13½ mile run to Dungeness. Driver, John Brice, can be seen just above the cab. Both this and sister locomotive *Doctor Syn*, which had originally been named *Black Prince*, were built to a Canadian style - the cab layout being more roomy than the previously built locomotives of more standard British style.

Above left: **HYTHE** At 28' in length *Winston Churchill* fits easily on the turntable at Hythe. Delivered to the railway in 1931 from The Yorkshire Engine Company of Sheffield, this loco was originally named *Doctor Syn*, after Russell Thorndike's renowned character from *Doctor Syn: A Smugglers Tale of the Romney Marsh*, published in 1915, and featured in a further six titles. She was renamed after the wartime leader just after the end of WWII. This view taken on 24 July 1975 shows her after conversion to oil firing in 1973. With the price of oil rising in the years that followed she was converted back to coal firing in 1979.

Mishaps can happen...

Right & below : **NORTH CAMP** A derailment on 8 July. While seemingly minor, with just one tanker off the rails, closer scrutiny indicates that the derailment was probably caused when the train failed to stop before hitting the buffer stops. Note the mangled railings between the last tank waggon and the storage tank. The potential for a major incident is clear with the close proximity of the storage tanks. The Surrey Fire Brigade have sent three tenders to the depot as a precaution, thankfully they were not called upon and the crews are clearly 'stood down'! The depot was adjacent to North Camp station which has changed names many times over the years! Opened in 1858 as North Camp, Aldershot, renamed Aldershot Camp in June 1863, then Aldershot, North Camp in May 1879. In June 1910 it became Aldershot North

Camp and South Farnborough, this lasted until July 1923 when it became Aldershot North, but only briefly as in March the following year it finally became North Camp as it is still known today. The fuel depot closed several years ago and local residents no doubt sleep a little easier as a result.

Left: **WIMBLEDON PARK** Heavy lifting gear has been brought in to attend to this derailment, the details of which were not recorded by the photographer - perhaps readers can throw some light on the circumstances? The crane nearest the photographer is a Cowans Sheldon with a lift capacity of 75 tons, while the second crane is capable of a 36 ton lift.

Below: **BETWEEN CLAPHAM JUNCTION & WANDSWORTH TOWN** This derailment took place on 19 December. The train involved consisted of 'Class 415/1'(4EPB) Unit No. 5131, built in 1954, leading, followed by Class 416/1 (2EPB) Unit No. 5675, built in 1959. The coaches from front to rear were Motor Second Brake, Trailer Second, Trailer Second, Motor Second Brake, Motor Second Brake, and Driving Trailer Open Second; all coaches were non-corridor. The complete train had a tare weight of 207 tons and a total brake force of 161 tons (77.6 per cent): its overall length was 387 ft. The official enquiry found that this derailment was the direct result of the removal of the bolts securing the stretcher bars to the open left-hand switch blade of the facing points in the Down Windsor through line at 4 miles 17 chains from Waterloo. This, together with either the failure to replace the scotch between the switch blade and stock rail, or the failure to replace it securely, enabled the switch blade to move from the fully open position to the fully closed position as the train passed over it, with the result that the rear bogie of the fifth coach and both bogies of the sixth coach were derailed. Thankfully none of the 50 or so passengers or railway staff were injured in this incident.

Depot Discoveries...

Below: WIMBLEDON EAST DEPOT

On 28 May Class 4EPB set No 5133, a complete 4 car set, stands in the lifting shop with a single unidentified Motor Brake Second Open from a sister set. The EPB (Electro Pneumatic Brake) sets were built at Eastleigh from 1951 to 1957 and the last of them were not withdrawn until as late as 1995. The cleanliness and neat and tidy appearance of the workshop is a stark contrast to the days of steam! There is just one 4EPB set in preservation, set No 5176, although at the time of writing it is split with 3 cars based at Northamptonshire Ironstone Railway Trust and the other, MBO, at Coventry Electric Railway Centre.

Crewe to a more powerful configuration and redesignated as 'Class 74' Electro Diesels. This did not fulfil all expectations and the new class only lasted 10 years, all being withdrawn by the end of 1977. Also 'on shed' are a pair of 4VEP sets.

Above: **WIMBLEDON EAST DEPOT**
Moving outside the depot on the same day, once again the overall cleanliness is in evidence. A variety of EMUs are 'on shed'. From left to right the two units inside the depot are a 4EPB (left) and a 2HAP. The ones outside in the stock sidings are 4SUBs.

Right: **ASHFORD CHART LEACON DEPOT** On 28 June, one of 24 Doncaster built Class 71s can be seen outside the shed. Built primarily for freight haulage these very successful locomotives were often to be found hauling *The Golden Arrow* and *The Night Ferry* an other passenger workings. Ten members of the class were converted during 1967 at

1975 Happenings (3)

September
- The Provisional IRA bomb London's Hilton Hotel killing two and injuring more than sixty.
- The Spaghetti House siege in Knightsbridge, London ends after six days with both robbers and hostages physically unharmed.

October
- Bill Clinton marries Hilary Rodham.
- Bomb explodes outside central London's Green Park tube station.
- Peter Sutcliffe, *The Yorkshire Ripper* commits murder for the first time.
- Prince Juan Carlos named Spanish Head of State as Francisco Franco's health deteriorates.

November
- First North Sea oil pipeline from Cruden Bay to Grangemouth is opened officially by H M The Queen
- Australian Prime Minister Gough Whitlam dismissed by Sir John Kerr the Govenor General. Malcolm Fraser appointed.
- Ross McWhirter is murdered outside his Enfield home after offering reward for information leading to the arrest of suspected terrorists

December
- The UK's *Sex Discrimination act* becomes law
- Icelandic North Sea patrol fires on unarmed British fishing vessel - the *Cod War* starts.

Below: **MARGAM DIESEL DEPOT** At 11.47am on a sunny 24 April, peace appears to reign as 'Class 37' 37217 rests to the rear of the depot between duties. Delivered in 1963 from English Electric's Vulcan Foundry as D6917, this loco was much travelled. Having been delivered new to Landore shed, it subsequently saw life at Stratford, Gateshead, Thornaby and Worcester depots, among others. Renumbered to 37127 in April 1974, withdrawal came in January 2006. A sale to HNRC followed in June of that year and at the time of writing had been moved to Barrow hill depot. An unidentified 'Class 47' hides amongst the barrels at the side of the depot.

MARGAM DIESEL DEPOT Minutes after the last view, Ray has moved into the yard outside this shed building. Surrounded by a mini-forest of the large light towers so redolent of modern facilities, 'Class 46' 46012 stands at the head of a short line containing an unidentified 'Class 47' and 'Class 37' together with two fuel tank wagons. The last 56 of the 'Peaks' built, the 46s had Brush generator and traction motors but were not as successful as the earlier models.

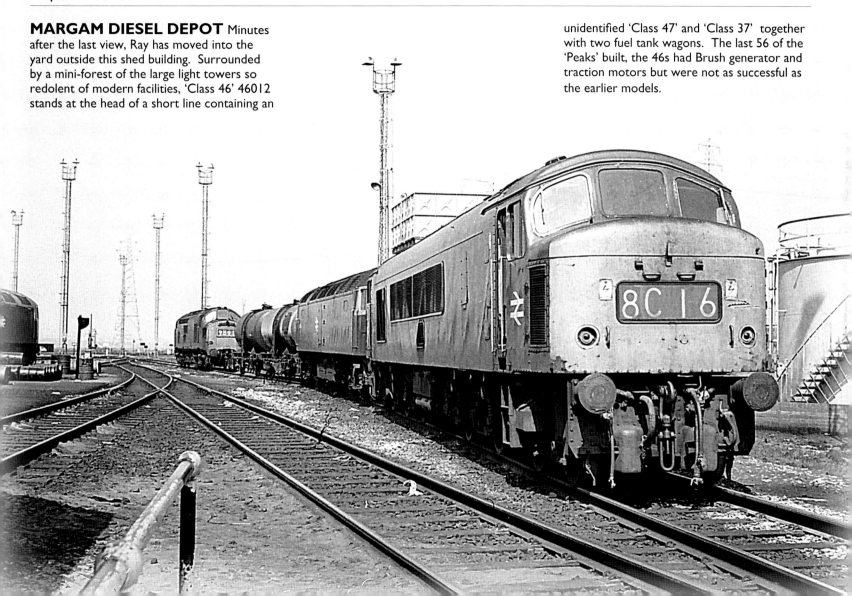

1975
No 1 Records

January
Lonely this Christmas	*Mud*
Down, Down	*Status Quo*
Ms Grace	*Tymes*

February
January	*Pilot*
Make me smile (Come up and see me)	*Steve Harley & Cockney Rebel*

March
If	*Telly Savalas*
Bye, Bye Baby	*The Bay City Rollers*

April

Bye, Bye Baby - stays at No 1

May
Oh Boy	*Mud*
Stand by your man	*Tammy Wynette*

June
Whispering Grass	*Windsor Davies & Don Estelle*
I'm not in love	*10 cc*

July
Tears on my pillow	*Johnny Nash*
Give a little love	*The Bay City Rollers*

August
Barbados	*Typically Tropical*
Can't give you anything (But my love)	*Stylistics*

September
Sailing	*Rod Stewart*

October
Hold me close	*David Essex*
I only have eyes for you	*Art Garfunkel*

November
Space oddity	*David Bowie*
D.I.V.O.R.C.E	*Billy Connolly*
Bohemian Rhapsody	*Queen*

December

Bohemian Rhapsody - stays at No 1

Winter Workings

Opposite above: **WIMBLEDON PARK SIDINGS** Following the initial launch of 'Britain's first all electric passenger main line' on 1 January 1933, the Southern Railway/Region EMUs have been progressively developed and updated. Predominant in this view from 7 July, is 'Class 421/2' 4CIG No 7377, one of the 4 car unit type introduced from BREL York in 1970. To its right 'Class 423' 4VEP No 7705 was slightly older having been one of the Class built at York and Derby from 1967 onwards. Interspersed between these more modern units are slightly older types introduced a decade or so previously.

Opposite below: **STAINES** In steam days views of carriages alongside main lines were a common sight. Obviously waiting for their next call of duty, many were 'abandoned' for long periods, sometimes for whole weeks with the only work being at weekends. Reduction in services, closure of lines and dieselisation, with the introduction of DMUs, as well as sheer economics, all brought the end to this scenario. Only on the erstwhile Southern system did the phenomenon exist to any extent with EMUs strategically parked awaiting the next job. Seen from a passing train, in November, unidentified units stand outside the depot.

Right: **Nr CROWTHORNE** Winter snow came late in 1975 but the falls were heavy enough to lead to highly decorative images. On 27 March, three-car unit 1202 stirs up powdery clouds as it heads south with an early morning Reading-Tonbridge service.

Below: **Nr CROWTHORNE** Slightly later in the day, on 27 March, even a degree or two warmer temperature has led to the snow falling from the trees and the sleepers between the rails emerging from their temporary burial. Consecutively numbered from the previous page, unit 1203 forms another Reading to Tonbridge service - this time the 1125 departure from Reading. As the photographer lived locally, one presumes he had returned home from the view of unit 1202, or he would by this time be VERY cold!

Nr CROWTHORNE Two more views of the snows between Crowthorne and Sandhurst.

Upper: A day later than already seen, three-car unit 1309 looks to have avoided a covering of snow on 28 March, perhaps by being inside a shed overnight, as it heads the 0734 Redhill-Reading duty.

Lower: Reverting to 27 March and the 0945 Tonbridge to Reading is captured during a snowstorm, peppering the front of the unit.

Left: **CROWTHORNE** More snow! Again captured during the frequent storms of 27 March, the driver of unit 1309 struggles to see through the flakes as he powers the 1024 Reading to Tonbridge service past Poflock Bridge.

Below: **CROWTHORNE** Another view from 28 March shows the aftermath of the snowstorms of the previous day. Seen from Brickfield Bridge, another Redhill-Reading service approaches, with early vestiges of the railway reappearing from beneath the white covering.

Right: **CROWTHORNE** Our final look at the 'seasonal' weather portrays 'Class 33' 33045 leading a decidedly mixed rake of coaches as the 1554 Rugby-Redhill inter-regional service on 27 March.

Index

Acknowledgements

First and foremost we would like to record our gratitude to the late Ray Ruffell without whom this book would not have been possible. Ray was a railwayman through and through and his interest went far beyond his day to day work, extending from miniature railways through narrow gauge to the most obscure industrial railways. Ray travelled the length and breadth of the British Isles and many locations abroad in pursuit of his subject.

Thankfully for us, and indeed future generations, Ray was also an accomplished photographer. His extensive collection has been kept complete and forms an important part of the photographic archives of *The* NOSTALGIA *Collection*. So many people have helped - with snippets and guidance, facts and information - space, and space alone, precludes mention of them all, so THANK YOU ALL!